GROW YOUR MIND

MAKE MISTAKES

Written by Izzi Howell
Illustrated by David Broadbent

CRABTREE
PUBLISHING COMPANY
WWW.CRABTREEBOOKS.COM

CRABTREE
PUBLISHING COMPANY
WWW.CRABTREEBOOKS.COM

Author: Izzi Howell
Series designer: David Broadbent
Illustrator: David Broadbent
Editor: Crystal Sikkens
Proofreader: Melissa Boyce
Print coordinator: Katherine Berti

A trusted adult is a person (over 18 years old) in a child's life who makes them feel safe, comfortable, and supported. It might be a parent, teacher, family friend, social worker, or another adult.

Library and Archives Canada Cataloguing in Publication

Title: Make mistakes / written by Izzi Howell ; illustrated by
  David Broadbent.
Names: Howell, Izzi, author. | Broadbent, David, 1977- illustrator.
Description: Series statement: Grow your mind | Includes index. |
  First published in Great Britain in 2020 by the Watts Publishing Group.
Identifiers: Canadiana (print) 20200222287 |
  Canadiana (ebook) 20200222473 |
  ISBN 9780778781707 (hardcover) |
  ISBN 9780778781783 (softcover) |
  ISBN 9781427125965 (HTML)
Subjects: LCSH: Failure (Psychology) in children—Juvenile literature. |
  LCSH: Failure (Psychology)—Juvenile literature. | LCSH: Errors—
  Juvenile literature.
Classification: LCC BF723.F27 H69 2021 | DDC j155.4/191—dc23

Library of Congress Cataloging-in-Publication Data

Names: Howell, Izzi, author. | Broadbent, David, 1977- illustrator.
Title: Make mistakes / written by Izzi Howell ; illustrated by David Broadbent.
Description: New York, New York : Crabtree Publishing Company, 2021. |
  Series: Grow your mind | Includes index.
Identifiers: LCCN 2020015547 (print) |
  LCCN 2020015548 (ebook) |
  ISBN 9780778781707 (hardcover) |
  ISBN 9780778781783 (paperback) |
  ISBN 9781427125965 (ebook)
Subjects: LCSH: Errors--Juvenile literature. | Decisions making--Juvenile
  literature.
Classification: LCC BF323.E7 H69 2021 (print) | LCC BF323.E7 (ebook) |
  DDC 153.1/524--dc23
LC record available at https://lccn.loc.gov/2020015547
LC ebook record available at https://lccn.loc.gov/2020015548

Crabtree Publishing Company

www.crabtreebooks.com   1-800-387-7650
Published by Crabtree Publishing Company in 2021

Published in Canada
Crabtree Publishing
616 Welland Ave.
St. Catharines, Ontario
L2M 5V6

Published in the United States
Crabtree Publishing
347 Fifth Ave.
Suite 1402-145
New York, NY 10116

Printed in the U.S.A./082020/CG20200601

First published in Great Britain in 2020 by The Watts Publishing
Group Copyright © The Watts Publishing Group 2020

CONTENTS

Mistakes and mindsets

When was the last time you made a mistake? It probably wasn't too long ago because everyone makes mistakes every day. It's a normal part of life.

How did you feel when you made the mistake? Maybe it was something like this:

> **I was so embarrassed and ashamed! I won't do that again.**

> **I'm glad I made the mistake because I can learn from it.**

One of these feelings comes from a **fixed mindset** and one comes from a **growth mindset**. Can you guess which is which?

People who are using a fixed mindset think their intelligence is fixed. They don't like making mistakes because they think mistakes mean they are a failure.

People who use a growth mindset understand that the brain is always growing and your intelligence can change. They know that making mistakes is a good way to learn.

Let's look inside the brain to understand how making mistakes makes your brain stronger.

Your brain contains billions of **neurons** that pass information to each other. Not all of your neurons are connected when you are born, but as you learn more things, you create new connections between them. This makes your brain stronger and more powerful.

Making mistakes is one way of creating new connections and growing your mind power, so don't be afraid to take risks and get things wrong! This book has all kinds of fun ways to help you learn how to develop a growth mindset and learn from your mistakes. So let's get started!

Feeling down

Some people feel disappointed or ashamed when they make mistakes. It's normal to feel that way, but you must not let these negative feelings get you down.

Be kind to yourself when you make a mistake. Talk to yourself in the same way that you talk to other people. Give yourself a brain hug by focusing on your good parts and giving yourself compliments.

Being mean to yourself about mistakes stops your brain from growing strong. Think of your brain as a blow-up ball. When you think negative thoughts, the ball deflates and the hard times can't bounce away. Thinking positively inflates the ball so that it can bounce away difficult moments.

Riya

I used to love painting. One day, I was working on a new painting of a horse and it came out all wrong. I felt so embarrassed.

I thought I was good at painting, so what happened? I knew I could start again, but I didn't want to. I was worried that the new painting would be bad as well.

Then my friend came over and looked at my painting. He said nice things about the colors and the way the horse was moving. I realized that I had been so busy looking at the parts I didn't like, that I hadn't noticed any of the good parts.

The next day, I started a new painting of a horse. I used the same colors and movement, but changed some of the parts that I didn't like from the first painting. It turned out really well!

THINK AGAIN

One way of being kind to ourselves when we make a mistake is to focus on the fact that we are learning, not failing!

Mistakes are steps on the path to success. A mistake can show us that an idea isn't correct, so we know we have to look for another solution.

Think about walking through a maze. When we reach a dead end, we turn around and try a different direction. Finding the dead ends helps us to find the way out and solve the maze.

All of the mistakes you make create new connections between neurons (see page 5) in your brain, which boosts your brain power! Try this activity to help you remember this.

On a piece of paper, write down a mistake that you made recently and how it made you feel.

Crumple the paper into a ball, getting out any frustration that you feel about the mistake.

Then, uncrumple the paper and trace along the folded lines with colored pencils. These lines represent the new connections made in your brain by making the mistake.

Keep the piece of paper someplace where you can see it. Whenever you look at it, it will remind you of how mistakes help your brain to connect neurons and get stronger.

Disappointed

Misspelled words on my spelling test

Types of mistakes

To learn from a mistake, it's useful to think about what type of mistake it is. We can sort mistakes into different categories.

A **slipup**—made because you were careless or not paying attention

A **blackout**—made because you forgot or didn't know important information

A **misread mistake**—made because you didn't read the question properly

An **active mistake**—made because you chose the wrong approach

For example, name the eight planets in the solar system.

Saturn

Uranus

Mars

Venus

Jupiter

can't remember (?)

Earth

Mercury

Which type of mistake has been made?*

We can use different strategies to
avoid different types of mistakes.

To avoid slipups, leave a few minutes at the
end to go over your work. Read it out loud
and see if you spot any obvious mistakes.

To avoid blackouts, you might need a different
study **strategy** to help you remember information
(see pages 12–13). If you don't know or understand
the information, ask for help! Asking for help is not
a weakness. It is a sign that you want to get better.

To avoid misread mistakes, take the time to read
the question carefully. It can help if you underline the
important words to make sure you focus on them.

To avoid active mistakes, you
may need more information
about the right approach, or
you may need to read the
question more carefully so you
choose the right approach.

*A blackout

11

A new strategy

Repetition is important when learning something new. Even if you understand it the first time, it will slip out of your mind unless you go back to it several times.

This is because studying what you've learned makes the connections between the neurons stronger so the information sticks in your mind.

Sometimes mistakes are a sign that you aren't studying in a way that suits your brain.

Everyone's brain is different, and can change over time. One day, writing things down might help you to remember. Other times, talking might help things to stick in your mind.

How do you study
when you have to learn
something new?

Try some of these other study techniques
and see how they work for you:

★ **Make flash cards.**

★ **Give a presentation to someone who
doesn't know anything about the subject.**

★ **Divide the information up into bullet points where
each bullet point is a different piece of information.**

★ **Draw a** mind map **with all of
the information that you can
remember. Then look back at
your notes and add anything
that you have missed.**

★ **Throw a ball back and forth
between you and a friend.
Each time you catch the
ball, say something that you
remember about the topic.**

Aha!

Sometimes mistakes are surprises. Have you ever thought you understood something until a mistake showed you otherwise?

This can be a shock, but think of it as an aha moment instead of a failure. **Trial and error** helps our brain make new connections so we can find the correct solution.

Think of it as a bunch of keys. Sometimes, you might have to try more than once before you find the one that fits and opens the door.

Jamie

Last week, we were taking turns reading a story aloud in class. When it was my turn to read, I noticed the word epitome in my sentence and I wasn't sure how to pronounce it.

I'd seen it written down before and I knew it was something to do with being the best example of something, but I wasn't sure how to say it.

I gave it my best shot and said it how I thought it was pronounced—ep-i-tome. A few people in the class started to giggle and I knew I'd said it wrong! My teacher explained that it was actually pronounced ep-i-ta-mee.

I felt silly in the moment, but then I noticed a lot of people were making mistakes when it was their turn. They were also learning how to pronounce words they had never heard said out loud before. Now I know how to say epitome and I won't forget!

A healthy brain

Sometimes we make careless mistakes. We might know the answer, but forget it because we aren't concentrating properly. This can happen when we don't take good care of our brains and our bodies.

Careless mistakes don't help your brain grow so you should try to avoid them.

Here are some ways to keep your brain and body healthy:

★ **Eat a balanced diet so your body has everything it needs to work well.**

★ **Eat regularly so your brain is powered up to learn.**

★ **Get enough sleep so your brain can rest and recharge for the next day.**

★ **Drink around five glasses of water a day so your body is well hydrated.**

★ **Take regular breaks so your brain doesn't get tired.**

Oliver

At lunchtime, I never used to eat all of my lunch.
I was too busy playing with my friends!

After lunch, I have science class. It's one of my
favorite subjects, but I would always get questions
wrong and forget what we learned the day before.

One day, it was raining so we couldn't go outside to play.
I ate my whole lunch, sitting and chatting with my friends.

That afternoon, my science lesson went so much better!
I worked really hard and understood everything.
I could even remember things later!

Now I eat my lunch before I go out to play.
This way, my brain has energy for the afternoon,
and I can work hard in science class.

Time to shine

When you are on your learning journey, it doesn't matter if you make mistakes. In fact, you should make them because it helps your brain to grow!

However, there are times when it would be a shame to make a mistake. It could be an important exam, a play or performance, or a sports game.

These aren't learning experiences—they are times to show off everything we know. It would be disappointing not to perform at our best and show off how much effort we have put in.

The best way to prepare for these moments is to go over any mistakes that you have made before.

Go through this checklist:

★ **Do you need any extra information? If so, what is it?**

★ **What have you done wrong previously that you could do differently this time?**

★ **How are you preparing? Does this method work well for you?**

★ **Is your brain well-rested and healthy before the big day?**

If things don't go as planned during the big event, don't be hard on yourself. Focus on what you can learn from the mistakes for next time.

TRYING NEW THINGS

Being afraid of making mistakes can make you afraid to try new things. You might think that if you end up making a mistake, it would be a sign that you can't ever be good at it.

But that's not true! Everyone makes mistakes when they try new things, and these mistakes help us learn.

Are there any activities that you've always wanted to do but have been afraid to try? Find a time to give them a try and see if you like them. Be prepared to make mistakes as your brain changes and learns how to do the new activity.

Adwoa

I always wanted to go to dance class.
Some of my friends went and it looked like so much fun!
But I have never gone because my friends are such
good dancers. I thought I would never be able to keep
up with them and I would make so many mistakes.

Then, last week, there was an open day at the dance school.
My friends convinced me to go along, so I did,
even though I felt scared I would mess up.

I did a trial class with lots of other beginners and I had so much fun!
I did make some mistakes, but so did everyone else around me.

I'm going to keep going to classes and working hard so that I
can catch up with my friends one day! Now, we practice their
routines together, even though it's hard for me to keep up.

Dancing is so much fun, I feel silly for
waiting so long to give it a try!

DON'T GIVE UP

Sometimes when we make mistakes, it can make us scared to try hard and make an effort.

We feel like we aren't making any **progress**, so why bother? You might feel like trying and failing is worse than not trying at all.

We can't let mistakes scare us away from trying, because learning requires effort. The hard work that you put in during the learning journey makes your brain stronger and helps to develop your skills.

Think about a personal goal that you worked really hard on. Choose something that makes you feel proud.

How did you achieve it?   **What mistakes did you make?**

What challenges did you face?   **How did you overcome the challenges?**

How did you feel when you found it difficult? What did you do?

Write down your answers and keep them safe somewhere. Now choose a new goal that you want to work toward. When the going gets tough, look back at your answers for inspiration!

Make the goal specific, as this makes it easier to work toward. For example, choose a goal such as "enter a photo I'm proud of in a photography competition," rather than "get better at photography."

Challenge o'clock

As we know, making mistakes
is one of the best ways to learn new things.
Instead of going for safe, easy activities,
we need to look for new challenges where
we will definitely make mistakes.

Pushing yourself to do difficult things is the best
way to grow your brain. Just as in sports, your
muscles have to work hard (and sometimes feel
tired and sore) to grow stronger. It's the same
with your brain!

Antonio

Last term, we could choose between two language classes at school—Spanish or Mandarin Chinese. My mom is Spanish so we speak Spanish at home.

I thought about doing Spanish because all my friends were going to do it. I knew the work would be easy and I'd be the best in the class!

But then I thought about it and realized it would be a waste of time to take Spanish, because I already know it! It would be so cool to learn Chinese, so I chose that instead.

It's hard work in class, and it took me a while to learn how to pronounce the different sounds. But I can already count to ten and talk about my family! I can't wait to learn more next term.

MY BEST MISTAKE

Looking back on past mistakes is a great way to learn in the future—they always teach us something.

We can also learn a lot from other people's mistakes. Sharing our mistakes shouldn't be something that we feel embarrassed about.

While you eat lunch with your friends at school, or dinner with your family, why not discuss the mistakes you made today and what you learned from them? Decide as a group who made the best mistake and why!

It could be someone who pushed themselves really far. Or it could be someone who put in a lot of effort and finally found a solution, after trying many different options and making a lot of mistakes!

You will always remember some mistakes, but there may be others that you forget over time. Why not turn a notebook into a mistake journal to track your best mistakes?

In the journal, write down mistakes that you have made and what you learned as a result. It could be new information, such as that the capital of the United States isn't New York, it's Washington, D.C.

Or it could be something that you learned about yourself. For example, you don't do well on your math homework when you do it while you watch TV, so you should do it somewhere quieter.

You could write in your journal every day or just save it for the really big mistakes that you don't want to forget.

Look back through the journal from time to time and congratulate yourself on all of the new things that you learned!

Famous failures

It's easy to think that famous people were born successful, but that's not the case.

A lot of people who went on to experience success did so as a result of hard work, and because they made a lot of mistakes.

Their mistakes motivated them to work harder, look at things differently, and keep going!

Life is kind of like the game of snakes and ladders. You will always encounter **obstacles** and mistakes on your path that set you back, but you have to keep on going to win!

Research a famous person that you look up to. It could be a business person, a musician, an athlete, or a politician. What was their path to success? Which obstacles did they overcome?

Turn your research into a poster. Hang the poster on your bedroom wall as a reminder that we all have to face failure and overcome obstacles on the path to success.

You could also talk to your teacher and ask if you could do this activity at school. You could hang the posters in your classroom to motivate others.

KEEP MAKING MISTAKES!

Read through this book's tips any time you need a quick reminder!

Don't be afraid to take risks and get things wrong.

It's normal to feel down when you make a mistake, but don't beat yourself up about it.

Remember that making mistakes helps to create new connections in your brain.

Thinking about the types of mistakes that you make can be useful.

Asking for help is not a weakness. If you don't understand, talk to your teacher, a friend, or an adult.

Studying in different ways can help us avoid mistakes.

Healthy brains and bodies are less likely to make careless mistakes.

Avoid mistakes at important events by planning first.

Don't let mistakes scare you away from trying, because learning requires effort.

You can't learn unless you challenge yourself, and new challenges often mean mistakes.

Don't be ashamed of your mistakes—share them with others.

Writing down your mistakes can help you learn from them.

Get inspired by famous people who have made a lot of mistakes on the path to success.

Glossary

fixed mindset   If you are using a fixed mindset, you believe that your intelligence is fixed and can't be changed

growth mindset   If you are using a growth mindset, you believe that your intelligence is always changing because your brain can grow stronger

mind map   A diagram with lines and circles connecting different ideas

neurons   Cells in your brain that pass information back and forth to each other

obstacle   Something that makes it difficult for you to do something

progress   Developing and improving your skills or knowledge

strategy   A plan that you use to achieve something

trial and error   Trying different things until you find one that works

Index

Notes for adults

The concept of a "growth mindset" was developed by psychologist Carol Dweck, and is used to describe a way in which effective learners view themselves as being on a constant journey to develop their intelligence. This is supported by studies showing how our brains continue to develop throughout our lives, rather than intelligence and ability being static.

Responding with a growth mindset means being eager to learn more and seeing that making mistakes and getting feedback about how to improve are important parts of that journey.

A growth mindset is at one end of a continuum, and learners move between this and a "fixed mindset"—which is based on the belief that you're either smart or you're not.

A fixed mindset is unhelpful because it can make learners feel they need to "prove" rather than develop their intelligence. They may avoid challenges, not wanting to risk failing at anything. This reluctance to make mistakes—and learn from them—can negatively affect the learning process.

Help children develop a growth mindset by:

- Giving specific positive feedback on their learning efforts, such as "Well done, you've been practicing…" rather than non-specific praise, such as "Good effort" or comments such as "Smart girl/boy!" that can encourage fixed-mindset thinking.

- Sharing times when you have had to persevere learning something new and what helped you succeed.

- Encouraging them to keep a learning journal, where they can explore what they learn from new challenges and experiences.

- Inspiring them to take risks, make mistakes, and reflect on lessons learned by sharing personal experiences and anecdotes.